Discovering

SONGBIRDS

Colin S Milkins

Illustrations by Wendy Meadway

The Bookwright Press
New York · 1990

Discovering Nature

First published in the
United States in 1990 by
The Bookwright Press
387 Park Avenue South
New York, NY 10016
First published in 1989 by
Wayland (Publishers) Limited
61 Western Road, Hove
East Sussex BN3 1JD, England

© Copyright 1989 Wayland (Publishers) Limited
Typeset by DP Press Ltd., Sevenoaks, Kent
Printed in Italy by G. Canale & C.S.p.A., Turin

Cover *A Marsh Warbler in full song.*

Frontispiece *A yellow-billed Magpie from California making an alarm call.*

Library of Congress Cataloging-in-Publication Data
Milkins, Colin S.
   Discovering songbirds / by Colin S. Milkins.
      p. cm.—(Discovering nature)
   Bibliography: p.
   Includes index.
   Summary: Introduces the characteristics and behavior of the approximately 4000 species of songbirds, describing how they sing, and discussing their migration, their enemies, and their friends.
   ISBN 0–531–18312–2
   1. Birds—Juvenile literature. 2. Bird-song—Juvenile literature. 3. Passeriformes—Juvenile literature. [1. Birds.] I. Title. II. Series.
QL676.2.M55 1990
598.8–dc20
89–32829
CIP
AC

Contents

1
Introducing Songbirds

This Californian White-crowned Sparrow is in full song.

What Is a Songbird?

There are about 9,000 species of birds. The largest is the flightless Ostrich, which is taller than a man, and the smallest is a tiny Humming Bird, no bigger than a bumble bee.

Most birds can utter some kind of song or just a simple call. But fewer than half of the 9,000 bird species can properly be called songbirds. It may seem odd, but songbirds are not grouped together because they all sing. Some do not. The cawing of a Carrion Crow or the screech of a Jay could hardly be called song, but both of these birds are technically songbirds. So what *is* a songbird?

The feature that all songbirds have in common is that they all have similar kinds of feet, that is, each foot has three toes pointing forward and one pointing backward. This is an excellent arrangement for gripping

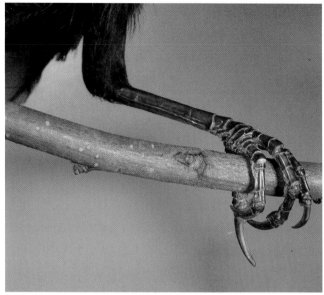

The brightly colored Jay is a songbird, although the loud screeching noise it makes cannot really be called song.

A Blackbird can grip a narrow branch with its four toes – three pointing forward and one backward.

narrow perches. It is for this reason that the songbirds are also known as the "perching birds." Lots of birds perch – eagles, parrots, doves and many more – but they are not called perching birds because the feet of the true perching birds are self-locking

and theirs are not. When a songbird settles down on a twig with its legs bent, its grip tightens automatically. This is very useful because the bird will never lose its grip and accidentally fall off its perch, even when it is fast asleep.

How Do Birds Sing?

Humans have a voice box in their throats called the larynx which enables them to speak. Songbirds have a larynx in the throat too, although it is not used to produce song, but just to make it louder. The part of the bird that actually makes the song is found down the windpipe inside the chest.

Where the windpipe divides to go into each lung, there is the "song box," or **syrinx**. Inside the syrinx there are two sheets of skin. On the outside, attached to the syrinx, are several sets of muscles. These muscles can continually alter both the shape of the syrinx and the tension of the sheets of skin. When the bird breathes out, air passes through the syrinx making the sheets of skin vibrate. This is how different notes are made. The two sheets of skin can be tensed

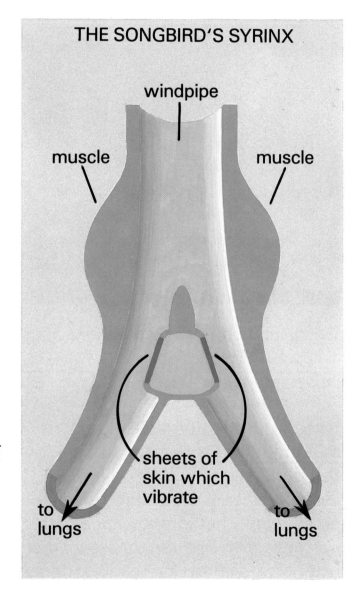

THE SONGBIRD'S SYRINX

windpipe

muscle   muscle

sheets of
skin which
vibrate

to
lungs   to
                          lungs

separately, which enables the bird to sing different notes at the same time. The notes and harmonies that are produced make up the bird's song.

Several songbirds can use the syrinx to mimic different sounds. The Indian hill Mynah Bird can imitate the human voice. Once, a soccer match had to be abandoned because of the chaos caused by a Starling imitating the referee's whistle. Mimicked sounds can help to make the male bird's song more varied, which increases his chances of attracting a mate. Mimicry can also protect birds. Jays for example will imitate the call of a Tawny Owl to frighten enemies away from their chicks.

Starlings are good mimics. They use their syrinx to mimic other sounds quite unlike their own rambling song.

Why Do Birds Sing?

In the spring the male bird takes up a **territory**. He sings both to attract a mate and to warn other males not to enter his territory. He repeats his song many times a day. Pied Flycatchers, for example, may sing up to 3,600 times a day. But the champion singer must be the Red-eyed Vireo who sings 20,000 times a day. Once a male has found his mate, he sings less often. For example, Pied Flycatchers may then sing only 1,000 times a day.

In most species it is only the male that sings. The Northern Cardinal is an exception. The female Cardinal sings as well and as often as the male.

The songs of male birds belonging to the same species are generally very similar, but slight differences enable a female bird to recognize the particular song of her mate.

Visual signals as well as song are important to some birds for keeping in touch when in a flock. The white outer tail feathers of Yellow Wagtails, or the prominent **wing bars** of Chaffinches flash when the birds are flying and tell the other members of the group "I am on the move again."

The Wren spends much of its time in dense undergrowth, so it needs a loud voice to be heard by other birds.

Birds that normally inhabit dense undergrowth have very loud songs because visual signals are less useful to them. The tiny Wren, which spends much of its time investigating dark holes and crevices at the bottoms of hedgerows, has one of the loudest bird-songs.

A White-browed Treecreeper flies from its nest displaying yellow wing bars, which act as a signal to other birds.

Bird Calls

Bird calls are important for communication. Individual birds within a flock will utter contact calls so that they will not lose touch with one another. For example, groups of Long-tailed Tits continually call "zee-zee-zee" as they flit from tree to tree. At night you may hear the calls of flocks of **migrating** birds high overhead. Unhatched chicks call to their parents and the parents reply, setting up a bond between them before the chicks hatch.

When the female is **incubating** her eggs, she will sometimes ask the male to feed her by making begging calls. This is because she cannot leave the eggs for long periods to look for food herself as the eggs would quickly become cold.

Alarm calls warn other birds when there is danger. The alarm call that warns of a hawk in the air is often different from the call that warns of a cat on the ground. Different species of birds that live in the same **habitat** may have similar alarm calls, so they can share information about a common enemy. Alarm calls are distinctive because they are usually short and sharp. This makes it very

A flock of Purple Finches feeds on the ground. They keep in touch with each other by constantly twittering. This is a form of "contact call."

A female Cedar Waxwing makes begging calls to her partner as she guards her nest.

difficult for a **predator** to locate the exact position of the bird that is giving the alarm call.

When a bird is caught by an enemy it gives distress calls. This generally frightens other birds and they fly away; but sometimes the birds in the area gang up on the enemy and try to drive it away.

Dawn Chorus and Dialects

The Nightingale often sings at night but most songbirds begin to sing as dawn approaches and the sky begins to lighten. **Ornithologists** have discovered that it is the increasing

Every morning at dawn, all the birds start singing. This is the dawn chorus.

amount of light and not the rise in temperature at this time that starts the birds singing. The early morning burst of singing from many different birds is called the dawn chorus. In Britain the first bird to start singing is the Blackbird, closely followed by the Song Thrush. One of the last to join in is the Whitethroat.

Songbirds may often be heard singing a very quiet, simple song that can only be heard within a yard or two. This type of bird-song is called a sub-song.

The song of a species differs from region to region. Although basically similar, the songs of northern Chaffinches are quite different from the songs of southern Chaffinches. Also, the song of the Winter Wren in North Carolina is different from the song of Winter Wrens living in the Hebrides Islands, off Scotland. These **dialects** have developed because separate populations of these birds have become isolated from one another. These dialects will, over thousands of years, lead to the

The song of the Chaffinch varies greatly.

development of completely different forms of song, and eventually the isolated populations may develop into different species.

2
The Bird's Body

A male Robin fluffs up his feathers, trapping a layer of warm air next to his skin to keep him warm.

Temperature, Breathing and Color

Birds have evolved from a small reptile-like creature called **Archaeopteryx** that existed some 150 million years ago. Birds still have some features of reptiles such as the scales on their legs and feet. Unlike the reptiles living today, however, birds are able to maintain a steady body temperature no mater how hot or cold their surroundings are.

To keep itself warm a bird fluffs out its body feathers to trap a layer of warm air next to the skin. That is why birds in winter often look fat and well fed, even though they may be starving. When a bird becomes too hot, it pants to speed up the removal of warmed air from its body.

Flying requires a great deal of energy. To obtain energy, muscles need lots of oxygen. When a bird breathes in fresh air fills the lungs,

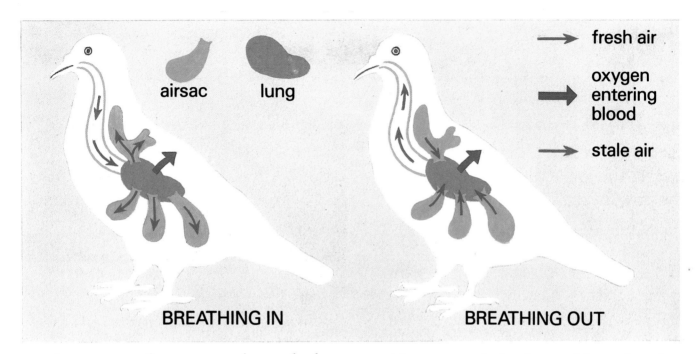

airsac lung

fresh air

oxygen entering blood

stale air

BREATHING IN

BREATHING OUT

and some air also passes through the lungs into special air sacs. The air sacs allow birds to absorb oxygen much more efficiently than mammals. When the bird breathes out, the fresh air from the air sacs enters the lungs and flushes out the stale air.

There are special pigments in a bird's feathers that give the **plumage** its colors. The brilliant sheens that

Unlike mammals, birds are able to absorb oxygen both when they breathe in, and out.

constantly change as some birds move are due to tiny wax prisms on the surface of the feathers. These prisms break up white light into the colors of the rainbow and this makes the bird seem to glow with multi-colored light.

Flight

The body of a songbird is well adapted for flight. In many birds the two enormous flight muscles make up half the bird's weight. These muscles supply the great strength needed for the downward stroke of the wings that gives the bird lift. Each of these muscles is attached to the **keel** of the breast bone at one end and to a wing at the other.

The shape of the wing overcomes the downward pull of gravity. Because the upper surface of the wing is more curved than the lower surface, air flows faster over the top than the bottom. Air pressure is, therefore, greater beneath the wing than on top, which makes the bird move upward.

Each wing has long flight feathers near the tip, which are called primaries, and shorter ones nearer the body, which are called secondaries.

This is a secondary feather. You can see clearly the individual barbs attached to the central shaft of the feather.

Attached to the central shaft of a feather, there are many barbs that together form the vane. It is important that the vane has a smooth unbroken surface for perfect flight. The barbs are prevented from separating by tiny interlocking hooks.

Birds keep their plumage in good condition by preening. To preen, the bird turns its head to collect oil from its preen gland at the base of the tail, and then it spreads the oil thinly over the feathers to keep them from becoming waterlogged. If the feathers became soaked with water, the bird would be too heavy to fly.

The bones of birds are hollow so as to be as light as possible for flight.

There are struts inside each bone, which give it a strength greater than a piece of steel of the same weight.

As this Reed Warbler's wings beat downward, the long primary, or flight, feathers spread slightly and the bird moves upward. The tail helps to steer the bird.

Bird Senses

Birds do not have a well-developed sense of smell. The senses of sight and sound are the most important. A songbird's eyes are on the sides of its head, and for this reason they are not very good for judging distances. It is the bird's excellent color vision

Birds have eyes that are very sensitive to color. By contrast, they have a poor sense of smell.

that makes up for this. Birds can judge distances by using the slight color differences in their surroundings as a key.

Most birds cannot move their eyes in the sockets, so they have to move their heads to look at something in front of them. You may see an American Robin cock its head at an angle when hunting for worms. It is not listening, but looking for worms.

Songbirds have very sensitive ears that can pick out the calls and song of their particular species from lots of similar noises. Ears also give the bird a sense of balance and position. This is very important when flying.

The ability of birds to taste varies a lot. In an experiment to stop birds from eating cherry blossom, the flowers were covered with the bitterest substance known to humans. Bullfinches took no notice of the bitter flavor and continued to eat them.

Birds can sense vibrations through their feet. When they are sitting on a perch they can detect a predator creeping up on them. This sense may also explain how some birds seem to know that an earthquake is about to happen. They may be able to sense

With one worm dangling in its beak, this hungry Blackbird cocks its head to look for another victim in the grass.

faint vibrations coming from the ground, hours before the earthquake actually happens.

3
Food and Feeding

This Tawny-colored Honeyeater is eating nectar from a flower.

The Bird's Gut

Birds do not have teeth, jaw bones or large muscles for chewing food. These structures would make their heads too heavy, and their bodies would be unbalanced in flight. They have a light, horny bill instead.

Birds are in danger from predators when they are feeding, so they gobble up their food, which is passed down the gullet into a storage bag called the crop. The food can then be digested when the bird is in a safer place. The food passes from the crop into the stomach where digestion begins. Birds need energy from their food quickly, so digestion has to be rapid.

The bird's "chewing" apparatus is part of the stomach called the gizzard. Birds that eat very tough food, such as seeds and nuts, have gizzards with thick, strong muscular walls. These muscles grind and churn the food.

Some birds swallow grit and small stones, which are kept in the gizzard to add to its grinding power.

Most birds cannot drink water by sucking it up with their mouths. They have to take in a beak full and then throw back their head. The water then trickles down the throat.

Birds get rid of their undigested food in their droppings. The droppings often contain living seeds, which will grow if they fall on soil. In fact, some seeds will not grow at all unless they have passed through the gut of a bird. Birds also remove a waste substance called uric acid in their droppings, which gives the droppings their white color.

A Greenfinch throws back its head to swallow water it has taken from a pool.

Types of Food

African Oxpeckers have sharp claws for clinging to the hides of mammals such as antelopes and oxen. The Oxpeckers are welcomed because they eat the flies and ticks that suck the blood of these mammals. In Britain, Pied Wagtails and fallow deer have been known to have a similar relationship. The Wagtails land on the deer's head and pick off the flies that collect around its eyes.

The Honeyeaters and Honeycreepers eat the **nectar** of flowers. Both of these types of birds have brush-like tips to their tongues for sweeping up the liquid nectar from the centers of the flowers. These Hawaiian birds are important **pollinators** of the plants they visit.

Crossbills are so named because of the way the upper and lower parts of the bill cross over at the tip. With a

An Oxpecker feeds on the flies and ticks it can find on the ears of an impala.

beak like this, a Crossbill can tear open the cones of larches and other **conifer** trees; they remove the seeds with their tongues. The **fledgelings** of the crossbill have straight bills. As the young bird matures once it has left the nest, the bill crosses over very gradually.

Hawfinches use their immensely powerful bills to crack open extremely hard cherry or olive stones to get at the seeds inside. Although this bird weighs only 50 gm (2 oz), it is able to exert a pressure of 72 kg (160 lb) with its bill. This would be roughly similar to the pressure that a man of average size would exert on your little finger if he stood on it.

This is the beak of a Honeyeater. Its fine, long, brush-like tongue sweeps up the liquid nectar from the flowers it visits.

Crossbills feed on the cones from conifer trees, using their strong crossed bill to break them open.

4
Reproduction

This Yellow-headed Blackbird is displaying his brightly colored plumage as part of his courtship ritual.

Courtship

When he has a territory, the male tries to attract and court a female. If she shows interest, the male sings and shows off in front of her. The male Blue Tit, for instance, performs the so-called "butterfly" display. He flies toward the female on outstretched, fluttering wings, more like a butterfly than a bird. He often has some food in his bill, which he gives to her as part of the courtship. As she accepts the gift she flutters her wings too.

The male and female of several species do not have the same markings. The male Snow Bunting, for example, has contrasting black and white wings. He shows them off by performing aerobatics above the female. Her wings are mainly brown with some white markings.

The male Bowerbird's courtship display is one of the most remarkable.

He builds a roofless tunnel of twigs called a bower and then collects many brightly colored objects, such as shells or feathers, which he places carefully around both entrances. Most of the objects are the same color as the female's plumage. If the bower is built near houses, bottle tops, colored glass and even gun cartridges may be used. Some males have been seen to paint a stick with colored berry juice. Then the bird struts around the Bower with the stick in its bill, hoping to impress the female. She usually watches from a distance.

Most songbird pairs separate at the end of the breeding season. But in some species, such as the American Chickadee and Wren, the pair remain together for life.

This Australian Spotted Bowerbird is collecting objects for his bower, in the background.

The Egg and Hatching

Mating begins with the male settling on the female's back. The **cloaca** of the two birds are brought together. Sperm will now pass from the male into the female to fertilize the eggs. After fertilization, a hard shell forms around each egg. Everything that the chick will need in order to grow is contained within the egg, except for oxygen. This gas passes from the air into the egg through the shell and collects in an air pocket.

Most songbirds lay four to six eggs, but the Firecrest lays a **clutch** of twelve. Birds that lead dangerous lives lay more eggs than those birds whose lives are less risky. For example, the continental Great Tit is a species that migrates. During this extremely hazardous journey many birds die, so to make up for this loss, the Great Tit lays two clutches a year.

A clutch of Blackbird eggs and one nestling. Like all songbirds, a Blackbird's young are born blind and naked.

Songbirds lay one egg each day. Once the clutch is complete the parents begin to **incubate** the eggs. During incubation the naked patch of skin on the bird's tummy is pressed against the eggs to keep them warm. In the female this patch of skin becomes red and inflamed, which increases the temperature. The skin in this condition is called the brood patch. The parents regularly turn the eggs so that they are warmed evenly.

After twelve days or a little more, the chicks are ready to hatch. The young bird rubs at the inside of the shell with its egg tooth until the shell breaks. The egg tooth, which is a hard structure at the tip of the bill, falls off a day or two after the chick has hatched out of the egg.

Below *The main parts of an egg.*

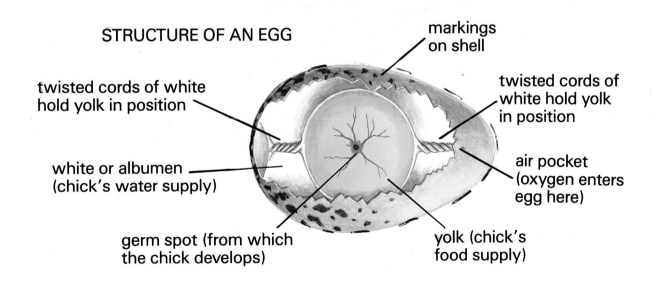

STRUCTURE OF AN EGG

markings on shell

twisted cords of white hold yolk in position

twisted cords of white hold yolk in position

white or albumen (chick's water supply)

air pocket (oxygen enters egg here)

germ spot (from which the chick develops)

yolk (chick's food supply)

Care of the Young

The newly hatched young of songbirds are blind and naked. The chicks have to be kept warm by the parents until their feathers grow, and they must be fed many times during the day. The Great Tit has been

The colored throats of these young Brewer's Blackbirds encourage the parent birds to feed them.

known to feed its young almost every minute from sunrise to sunset. In many species the chick's colored throat patterns encourage the parents to push food into its mouth. When a model of a chick with a large mouth and painted throat was placed beside a nest that contained real chicks, the parent birds fed the model.

A chick that has just been fed settles back into the bottom of the nest for a short sleep. The next time one of the parents returns with food, a different chick will be fed.

The chick's waste is not passed as normal liquid droppings because that would quickly foul the nest. The chick raises its rear end and passes a tough little bag of waste called a fecal sac. These are either eaten by the parents or dropped away from the nest. Fecal sacs are white, and if they were dropped near the nest they would attract the attention of predators.

A parent Great Tit takes from the nest a fecal sac containing the chick's waste.

After leaving the nest the fledgelings are still dependent on their parents for food for up to a week or ten days.

Young birds are not taught to fly by their parents. They just grow into it. A few weeks after leaving the nest they are able to fly as well as their parents.

Nests

Although the nests of some songbirds are simple cup-shaped structures, other species build elaborate nests using a variety of materials. Oven-birds in South America, for example, use wet clay to build their nests, which are often placed on top of posts. The clay bakes hard in the sun, which makes it impossible for an animal to break into it. Would-be robbers, such as snakes, find the spiral-shaped entrance difficult to get through.

Nuthatches nest in cavities of old trees. They use mud to make the entrance hole oval shaped so that it is a tight squeeze to get in. Rufous-throated Thornbirds protect their

Left *This large nest was built by Social Weaver birds in Namibia, West Africa. It is cleverly built into the branches of the tree, using grass and clay.*

nests by building them with sharp, thorny twigs. More than one pair of these birds share the building of a large **communal** nest. The finished structure may have separate compartments for each breeding pair.

Another species that nests together is the Social Weavers. The individual nests are joined together to form a single structure, which can fill a whole tree. Weavers tie special knots to join grass stems to the branches of the tree. This careful construction makes the community of nests very strong.

Some birds use trickery to protect their nests. Cape Penduline Tits make an enclosed, hanging nest. At the side of the nest there appears to be a large, inviting entrance hole, but it is nothing more than a blind pocket that leads nowhere. A predator becomes totally confused when investigating this false entrance; the real entrance is much less obvious.

A Penduline Tit returns to its nest to feed its young. The huge nest, woven from grass stems, hangs from the branches of a tree.

5
Migration

The Redwing is a Thrush that migrates to Britain from Scandinavia during the winter months.

Where Do They Go and Why?

Not all songbirds migrate, but those that do make the long journey twice a year. Birds that breed in the north migrate south after their young have fledged. In the following spring they make the return journey. Young birds that have never made the journey before know the way by instinct. They are not shown the way by their parents, who often leave before them. All migrant birds may find their way by the position of the sun and stars.

Most birds migrate because food becomes scarce at certain times of the year. For example, the swallow cannot remain in its northerly breeding grounds for the winter because the insects on which it feeds will die.

So why do birds bother to migrate north at all? Why don't they stay in the south where insects can be found at all times of the year? The answer is that the parents need the extra daylight hours of the northerly summers to gather enough food for themselves and their chicks.

Some species know when to migrate because of seasonal changes in temperature. Others migrate as the amount of daylight changes, when one season gives way to another.

Before they migrate, birds fatten themselves up on insects or berries, which are rich in sugar. The stored food in the form of fat provides migrating birds with energy during their long, hard journey.

Songbirds often gather together before they migrate, as these swallows are doing.

6
Enemies and Friends

This Jay is using ants to get rid of the lice and other parasites living among its feathers.

Who Are Their Enemies?

In many parts of Europe, songbirds are shot for sport. They are also eaten as delicacies. Some birds that have lovely songs are captured with nets or by **liming** a favorite perch, and then caged for entertainment.

A far more serious threat to songbirds is the destruction of their habitat. Woodlands and forests are being cut down for lumber and development.

Sparrowhawks kill many songbirds. While in flight the hawk reaches out with its very long legs to snatch the terrified bird. The hawk does not kill its prey with its bill but squeezes it with its **talons**. Magpies and Jays kill and eat many nestlings and also take eggs. The Woodpecker breaks open nest boxes and eats the chicks inside. Domestic cats are a serious threat to birds, too. They will often just play with a captured bird until it dies.

Bloodsucking by lice and fleas is a nuisance to adult birds and can be serious enough to cause the death of nestlings. In spring, fleas can be seen around nesting cavities waiting to jump on the first bird that enters.

One way that birds have found to remove parasites is anting. Two or three living ants are carefully picked up in the bill and rubbed along the feathers. The furious ants squirt out formic acid, which is strong enough to dislodge lice. Crows sometimes use discarded burning cigarette ends or a glowing twig from a bonfire to remove parasites.

Domestic cats are a common threat to songbirds, often playing with the birds until they die.

Helping Songbirds

Clean feathers are essential if birds are to stay warm in the winter. Birds keep their plumage in good condition by bathing early in the morning and later in the day before they go to **roost**. In

Below *A Coal Tit and a Blue Tit enjoy eating peanuts from a feeder.*

Above *Nest boxes should be made of thick pieces of wood to insulate the young chicks from extremes of temperature.*

the winter natural water supplies often freeze. You can help birds during winter by giving them ice-free water for bathing and drinking.

The best way to provide water is in a metal tray supported on four bricks. A burning "night light," which is a short candle, can be placed underneath the tray. The gentle heat from the flame will keep the water from freezing. Never put anti-freeze in the water as it will kill the birds. If you have a pond, lay a branch on the bank with some of the twigs dangling in the water. Songbirds will land on the branch and hop down the twigs to drink the water.

Food such as peanuts, kitchen scraps, raisins, mealworms and fat will be readily eaten by many types of birds. Peanut butter is a favorite of several American birds and is worth trying in your own yard. It is safer not to feed birds during the breeding season. They will sometimes give their chicks unsuitable food, which could kill them. Remember not to place water or food near a fence or bush where a cat could lie in wait.

Nest boxes are always welcome, especially by the tit family. Make the boxes of wood, with a hole 28 mm (1 in) wide. Tits will peck around the entrance hole and at the sides of the

It is important to supply water for birds in winter. This Blackbird has found an unfrozen pool to drink from.

box when they are inside. They are not trying to make the hole bigger. They are making sure that the wood is not rotten. A nest box or natural cavity of decaying wood could be damaged in a spring gale, which might be dangerous for the eggs or chicks.

7
Learning More About Songbirds

The Nightingale has a rich, loud, and musical song. It sings during both the day and the night.

If you find a skeleton of a bird look for the keel on the breast bone. Pull away one of the long bones and carefully file away the surface to reveal the strutting inside.

Recordings of bird song can now be obtained on tape and disk. Listen to them carefully and after a while you should be able to identify the songs that you hear when you are out studying birds.

When spring comes, get up some day before dawn. Sit quietly and make a note of the time and order that the different birds start to sing. If you do this on a clear day and then on a cloudy day, you will be able to note whether the time that the birds begin to sing differs at all.

Later in the season carry out a breeding survey. Make a rough map of the area you want to survey and mount it on a clip board. Walk slowly around the area. Mark on the map the

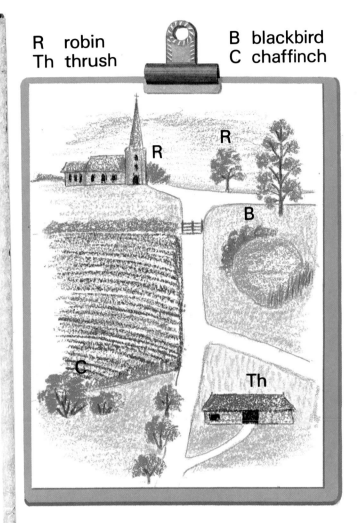

R robin
Th thrush
B blackbird
C chaffinch

This is a simple plan for a breeding map. The letters on the map show the places where male songbirds were heard singing.

position and the species of any singing male that you find.

There are several signs of breeding to look for, such as parent birds trying to distract your attention from their nest, alarm calls from the parent birds, adult birds carrying food or fecal sacs, or begging calls of young chicks. Remember, if you think that there is a nest nearby, do not go near it. If you disturb the nest, the parents may desert their young or the eggs.

The best way to study birds is from a distance using binoculars – 7 × 35 binoculars are the best. Locate the bird with the naked eye first. Without blinking or taking your eyes off the bird, even for a fraction of a second, raise the binoculars to your eyes. This technique usually brings the bird into view the first time. Whatever way you choose to study birds, remember always to put their interests first and your own second.

Glossary

Archaeopteryx (pronounced arkeyopteriks) A bird-like reptile that lived 150 million years ago and had feathers, teeth, a bony tail and no keel. Its flight was probably just short glides.

Cloaca The sexual opening of male and female birds. It is also the opening through which droppings are passed out of the bird's body.

Clutch A set of eggs that are laid together.

Communal Living and breeding together as a group.

Conifers Trees that have needle-shaped leaves and cones.

Dialect A different form of a basic song.

Fledgeling A young bird that has just left the nest.

Habitat The area in which an animal or plant lives naturally.

Incubating Keeping eggs warm by sitting on them.

Keel The thin piece of bone jutting out from the breast bone.

Liming Painting a sticky substance called lime on a perch. When the birds land on the perch they become stuck and cannot fly away.

Migrating Moving from one place to another and back again at particular times of the year.

Nectar A substance rich in sugar produced by some flowers to attract pollinators such as bees.

Ornithologists People who study birds scientifically.

Parasites Animals that live and feed on other living things.

Plumage All of the bird's feathers.

Pollinator An animal that accidentally carries pollen from the male part of a flower to the female part of another flower. Without pollinators some plants would not be able to reproduce.

Predator An animal that catches and kills other animals for food.

Roost A place where birds go to sleep for the night, often in flocks.

Syrinx The part of the bird that produces its song.

Talons Sharp claws of birds of prey.

Territory The area in which one pair of birds will breed.

Wing Bars Markings on the wings of certain birds.

Finding Out More

If you would like to find out more about songbirds, you could read the following books:

Carolyn Boulton, *Birds*, Franklin Watts, 1984

J.I. Dunn and Eirik Blom, *Field Guide to the Birds of North America*, National Geographic Society, 1983

George S. Fitcher, *Birds of North America*, Random House, 1982

For more information on other birds read:

Anthony Wharton, *Discovering Sea Birds*, Bookwright, 1987

Anthony Wharton, *Discovering Ducks, Geese and Swans*, Bookwright, 1987

Some useful addresses

National Audubon Society
950 Third Avenue
New York, NY 10022

The Audubon Society may be able to tell you about recordings of songbirds in your local area.

Index

Tawny-colored Honeyeater
  24, 26, 27

White-browed Treecreeper
  13
White-crowned Sparrow 8

Whitethroat 17
Wing bars 12, 13
Wren 12, 13, 18, 29

Yellow Wagtail 12

Picture Acknowledgments

All photographs are from Oxford Scientific Films by the following photographers: George Bernard 12; Mike Birkhead 18, 23; Ennio Boga 35; Neil Bromhall 33; Michael Brooke 34; John Gerlach (Animals Animals) 15; Philippe Henry 16; Michael Leach 21, 41; Ted Levin 40 (right); G.A. Maclean 25, 36, 40 (left); Colin Milkins 9 (left), 20, 22, 39; Patti Murray 37; Stan Osolinski 28; Richard Packwood 30; Charles Palek (Animals Animals) 32; C.M. Perrins 27 (right); Rafi-Ben-Shahar 26; D.J. Saunders 38; Frank Schneidermeyer frontispiece, 8; Marty Stouffer (Animals Animals) 14; Barry Walker 9 (right), 11, 17; Babs and Bert Wells 13, 29, 24, 27 (left).